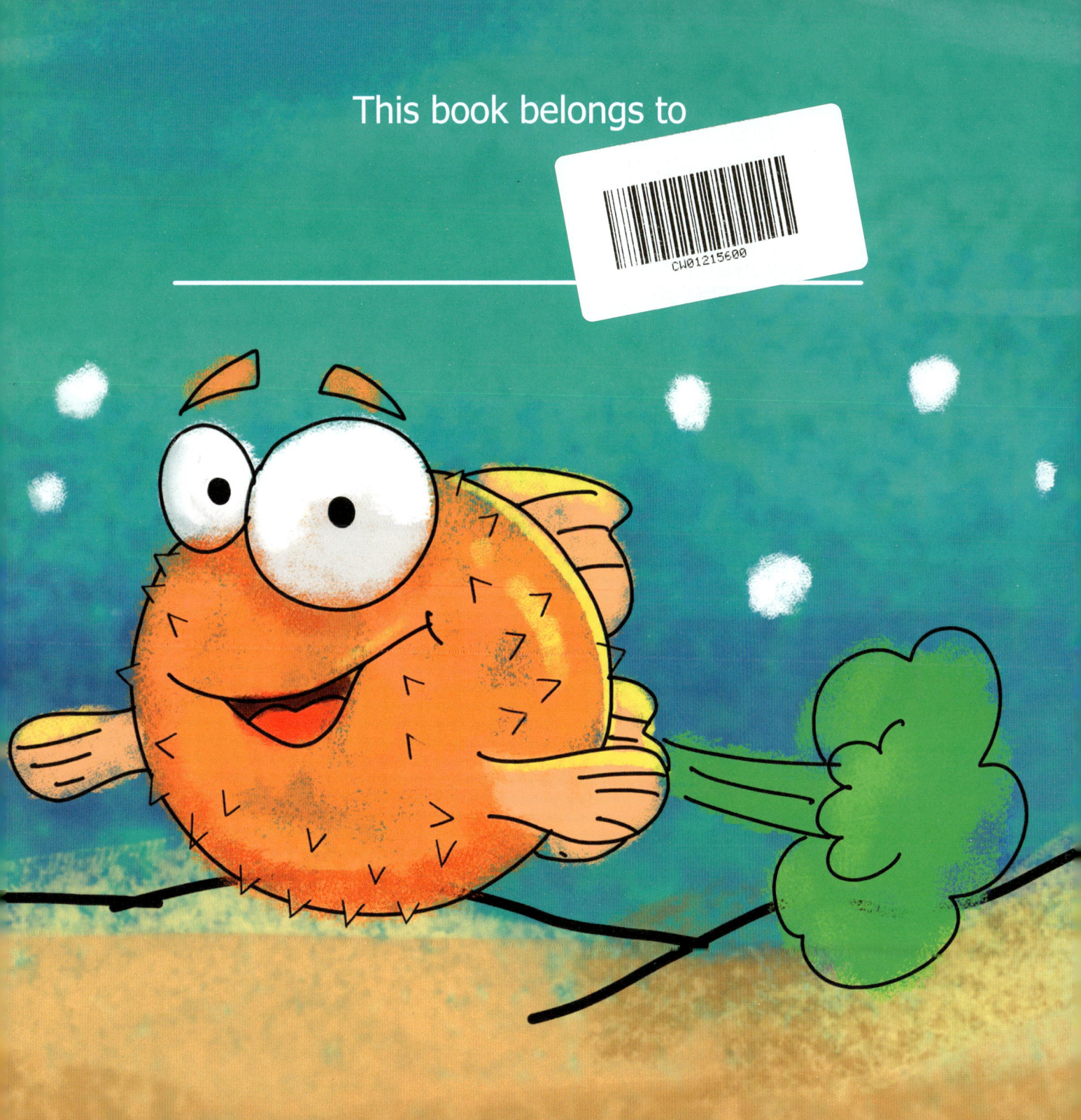

Copyright © 2021 by Humor Heals Us. All rights reserved. No part of this book may be reproduced in any form without permission in writing from the publisher. Please send questions and requests to humorhealsus@gmail.com Printed and bound in the USA. 978-1-63731-039-7 Humorhealsus.com

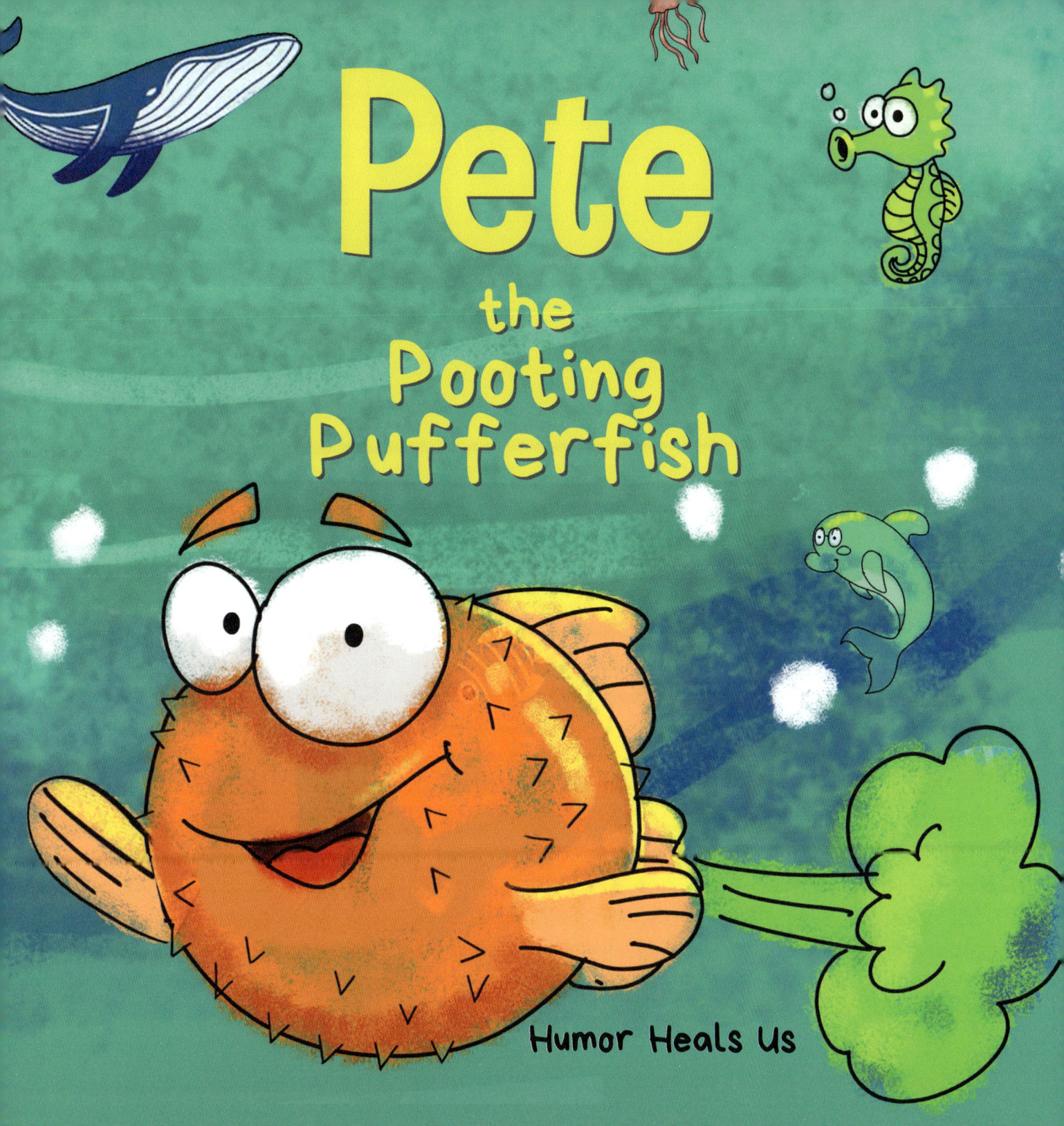

I know I'm weird,
And kind of gnarly.
Even though
I'm very pooty.

Pete the pooting pufferfish...
It's my nickname.
If someone stunk up a room,
I'm always the one to blame.

Did you know
Today's my birthday?
And I have only one wish,
If I may.

To have a true friend,
Through and through.
One that stands by you
No matter what you do.

Everyone experiences gas,
I can't be the only one.
I feel so good
When I'm done.

I admit sometimes
I can stink it up.
I wouldn't mind smelling
Like a peanut butter cup.

Maybe what I should do is
Hold in the gas.
But I'd probably blow up into a balloon
Oh so fast!

This can't be the solution.
This can't be the way.
I must find another answer.
Wouldn't you say?

All I have to do is
Follow the smells.
Look! What's down there?
Near the seashells...

Would you like to be friends,
Oh, dear crab?
Ouch! Please don't hurt me,
Please don't stab!

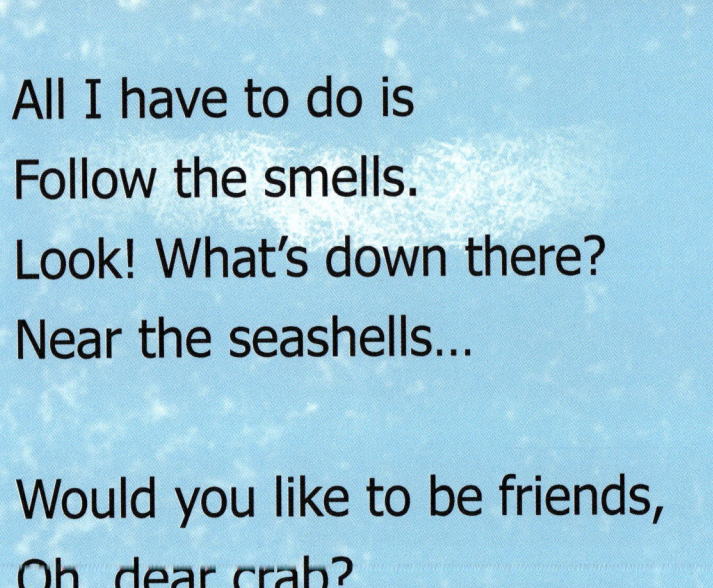

I swim over to the dolphins
But they won't talk to me.
I ask the octopus if he'll play.
But he says, "Leave now. Let me BE!"

I won't give up.
I must stay the course.
Will you be my friend,
Please, sea horse?

Instead, he kicks me
To the dark waters nearby.
I say hello to the blue whale
As I fly.

The turtles are bathing
In the sun.
They lay on me
And I can't run.

Should I pay a visit
To the great white shark?
That's probably not a good idea
Since it's dark.

Past the school of fish,
I swim.
Until I reach where
The light is dim.

Here is where
The jellyfish live.
But friendships are not
What they want to give.

I can't believe
In this whole wide sea.
I can't find
One pooting friend like me.

I'm out of luck
I give up hope.
I hadn't one friend.
And all I can do is mope.

Wait, what's this?
A birthday party invitation today.
Hmmm...What's the party for?
It doesn't say.

The location is near the coral reef
Where the seaweed is furry.
I bet I can still make it,
If I hurry!

I might get kicked out
So I pray.
But then to my surprise,
Everyone sings me happy birthday!

I'm so lucky,
I'm so grateful.
I can poot,
I'm not fearful.

I do have true friends.
They accept me for who I am.
Because every one
Can be a gem.

Printed in Great Britain
by Amazon